Lye

Sunshine Lately

Fernwood PRESS

Lye

Fernwood Press
Newberg, Oregon
www.fernwoodpress.com

Printed in the United States of America

Page design: Mareesa Fawver Moss
Cover design: Brian Ott
Author photo: Nearly Lemon

ISBN 978-1-59498-219-4

Through epigrammatic memories and cinematic scenes, the poems in *Lye* recover moments of developmental trauma to re-author a powerful self-mythology. It is a self-mythology that transforms, like ash and water, through organic material, chemical reactions, and electric epiphany. Sunshine's voice moves from innocent to caustic to easeful across the poem's three sections and the old narrative—it's punitive, paternal, and biblical limitations—is cleansed away. In turn, they become the "creator / of (their) own bright and / terrifying world." I'm warmed by this Kentuckiana poet and the spirit in their poems!

—Joy Priest
author of *Horsepower*

How is a daughter shaped, when the border between intimacy and violence is razor thin? When "touch is only ever / a sexual invitation" and conversations are laced with dread? In a family where men happen to women like catastrophes? She is shaped with "sweat and ash." Needing to be "born / again and again." She becomes "a dual / spirit, split and burning," a "pale and terrified stranger." However *Lye* is not only a coming of age story but a survivor's tale. Lately's speaker survives by recognizing that "hurt daughters become / hurt mothers" and "This is the truth / every daughter must swallow: / *only we can save ourselves.*" They heal into their whole self by finding an alternative path from "our line / of mothers / who believed every word their fathers said." *Lye* is a book about toxic fathering and self-rescue. Readers will want to hang on to the very end to discover "What grows / in the garden / at the end of the world." A fierce and fearless debut.

—Jill Khoury
author of *earthwork*

Lye holds up a mirror to the journey taken to reach the deepest parts of ourselves. Sunshine Lately combines memory with poetic processing in such a way that you travel, not only through pages but also through self. May we always remember the liberating power of honesty. *Lye* is liberation, self-discovery, and a portal to what is possible when one chooses to take the journey through it all.

—Korie Griggs
author of *Suffer Well: Poems for the Grieving*

Just as toxicity and remnants of burning can be combined to create something that washes things clean, the poems in *Lye* use the raw material of generational trauma to chronicle a journey toward love and hope. With honest, clear vision, *Lye* traces the fallibility and failures of family and shimmers with the strength of a new self forged in their wake. These poems—like oil, lye, and ash—flow, sting, and burn as they cleanse.

—Donna Vorreyer
author of *Unrivered*

I read Sunshine's *Lye* in one great gulp and came up gasping for air, cheering and weeping. From the opening preface to the epilogue at the end, I was gripped by this story of resilience and survival. Lately speaks to their mother, "I wish you would have lived with nothing in your belly but lightning." And by the end (spoiler alert), Lately realizes "all I have to do is become something electric now." And they do—this book is electricity itself. "Keep telling me to be quiet," Sunshine says, "Then pull the lever and see if you'll get cherries or bombs."

—Joann Renee Boswell
author of *Meta-Verse!: it's going to be interesting to see how yesterday goes*

for Emily,
for carrying me

Contents

Sodium hydroxide, a prologue

In liquid form, lye
is odorless and colorless.
My sorrow knows
this chemistry–
how fierce burning can be
otherwise undetectable.

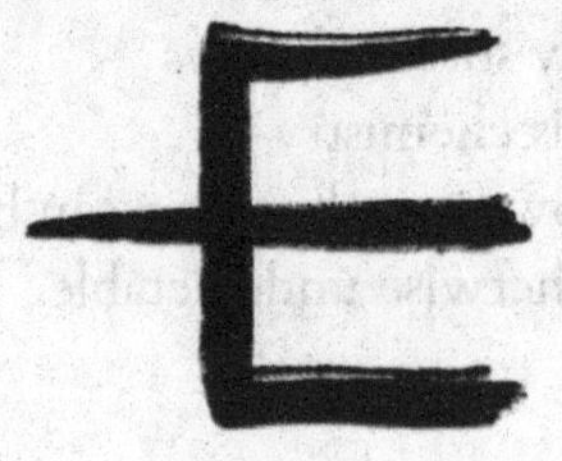

ash

I am but carbon
and grief.
A palace fired
to its bare scaffolding,
groaning into
the collapsed posture
of anguish.

I can only imagine him

heavily.

Heavy, as the weight he was given,
swallowed and passed
along to women who were only taught
how to carry.

Heavy, as any man
who was once a lonely boy
before he buried grief
in his belly and loaded
burden on his back.

Heavy, as the leaded fuels
of pride and revenge–
propelling as they are
debilitating.

Heavy, as my loss
of soft paternity, the easy
you've-got-a-friend father
he said he would be.

But my father,

My father is John Wayne,
savior of women and virtue.

My father is God Himself,
all alpha, no omega.

My father is Santa Claus,
elusive judge and voyeur.

My father is a son of a bitch
who taught him too little of love.

I can only imagine her

lightly.

Light as her fluffed curls,
her youthful penny-loafered steps,
or her decisions yet made like
virgin dynamite wicks: unlit.

Light, as a woman is always light
before she grabs the falling
rope and anvil
of a man.

Light, as in *faint*,
as in the way
I see the life she could have lived,
as flour clouds puff,
drift, then fall away
from working hands
before completely losing
their shape.

But my mother

My mother is Cleopatra,
at the foot of her own throne.

My mother is the Moon,
emptied every day.

My mother is Athena,
hiding peace behind her shield.

My mother is Lilith,
the first wife no one talks about.

When did they stop asking about you, Mama?

As I became greater,
you became less.

Perhaps in this way,
all women are mothers:
defined only
by what we carry.

You carried me,
and I carry grief.
And as both become greater,
we become less.

I never asked to be here.
I wish you would have lived
with nothing in your belly
but lightning.

Bitter as the tea

I did not choose
the time or place, or mother or father,
or the position
of the sun or moon or stars,
or the cortisol
that coursed Mama's blood and mine,
or the propensity
for nearsightedness and crooked teeth,
or this hot ancestral ache
like a toxic tea
that brewed for centuries before I ever
took a sip.

I came into the final chapter
of a tale written by generations
of tired women— written
with sharp quills licked and dipped
into the ink they made
from their own sweat and ash.

June 14, 1990

Mama and I were both born

under waning gibbous moons.

Among the spiritualists

who study the stars, this lunar phase

is known to predispose its children

to a life of introspection and rebirth.

That bloody evening, the moon moaned

her prophecy. Since then,

Mama and I poured our decades

into learning its truth:

we will be born

again and again and, yes,

new life's first feeling

is terror.

INTRUSIVE MEMORIES: SCENE 1
TRAILER PARK, INDIANA,
HER BEDROOM - 1993 - MORNING

She (3yo) lays on her back on her bed, wearing an oversized, tie-dye Little Mermaid nightshirt. Her knees are propped up, with the heels of her feet on the edge of the mattress. She is breathing rapidly and loudly, per Dad's direction, as if in labor, with a confused look on her face.

CUT TO:
He (24yo) is holding her knees apart, breathing with her as if he was a birth coach.

HIM:
Push! 1,2,3, PUSH!

BACK TO:
She grunts in pretend play, doing as she's told.

CUT TO:
He pulls a baby doll from the belly of her shirt and holds it up triumphantly.

HIM:
It's a girl!

Misogyny and middle names

How long after marveling
at my innocence, bound, did you begin
to deliberate my name?

Petitioning against
Abbigail May, saying
you could already hear
the boys sing about me:

Abby May,
Abby Might,
Abby Probably Will.

You held the culmination
of your ancestors
in a bundle and then
remembered man's hunger
as presently as the spit
that built in your mouth?

When I say god is a woman, I mean

god is the blood and bone
of a mother's open hips
unhinged, permitting
the truest expression of life:
cries. I hear god
in the memory of those
pained bellows.
I was there, I passed through
god, but
I too was crying.

I mean men
don't understand
this blood and bone,
the warmth they fell from—
once so enveloped in softness
and skin, and then
the womb's warmth
drains from them.

So men
build fires and forget, create
god again in their image and obsess
over the open hips of women
without remembering why.

INTRUSIVE MEMORIES: SCENE 2 TRAILER PARK, INDIANA, LIVING ROOM - 1994 - MID-MORNING

He (26yo) sits at his computer desk stationed in the living room of their mobile home. He is playing Duke Nukem, intensely focused, with little attention to spare. A lit Marlboro Light hangs in the ashtray next to a crushed Mountain Dew can on the desk.

CUT TO:
She (4yo) hides under the desk by his feet. She wears patterned cotton leggings and a pink shirt with this morning's syrup crusted along the neckline.

HER:
Do you think God can see me here?

HIM:
Yep.

CUT TO:
She wears an excited and curious grin as she quickly hides under the coffee table behind him.

HER:
What about here!

BACK TO:
He doesn't break his gaze from the monitor. His face remains expressionless until suddenly he winces as he narrowly misses being shot by an opponent in-game.

HIM:
Shit! Yep.

CUT TO:
She runs to the kitchen with quick and heavy steps. Her messy blond hair falls into her face before she pushes it back with the palm of her hand. She hides under the half-wall counter between the barstools. Her grin has now grown to a mischievous, excited smile.

HER:
What about h-

HIM:
Yes, dammit. He can see you everywhere.

Quantum physics asks

Does an item have features
until they are measured
by man?

The cavern in my belly and the god
named after me both echo:

no

The god created in my image
barely exists. We are the space
between words, the findless line
within gender, the shape of a bite
sucked from any fruit, a metaphor
for anything both *there* and *gone*,
an item behind the veil, a fullness
poured from a finite container.

Frail

A cigarette left unattended
still burns.
Its white ashes hold
their shape as long
as they can, and
I think I have been
that cigarette before.

Both arms

Dad twisted Mama's arm in the parking lot of a church
on the night of my ballet recital. Before that, he slept

with a nineteen-year-old girl he called Jackie. I don't know why,
because Jackie wasn't her name. Dad met Jackie

at the grocery store where he worked. He worked
at the grocery store because he said other things mattered

more to him than conventional success. I think if he said
the quiet part out loud, he'd say *third shift is really great for sleeping*

with Jackie. The morning of my ballet recital, Mama
woke me up tenderly. She deserved a *good morning,*

but instead I asked, *Is today the day? Can I wear it?*
Like I'd asked in my first waking seconds of many days

before that. I was talking about my ballerina dress: the crushed
velvet, silver sequins, and pink tulle I coveted, which hung high

in my closet for weeks. I thought about that dress as fervently
as my dad salivated for Jackie. That night, after my recital,

Mama tucked me in with both arms. And I probably said
something ignorant like *goodnight* instead of *how is your arm* or

is there a single person in this world
who sees you?

Appliance

The kitchen
is the working room.

The kitchen
is where the woman
belongs.

Wash her when you're done
using her.

Store her carefully between
the knives and cutting boards
until you get hungry
again.

Was she happy before me,
or never at all?

I took my mama's worth and traded it
for postpartum weight.

Once, the world cooed to me
through her belly.

But now that she's dispensed me,
she's dispensable, too.

And now that I'm here, that belly
gets no love.

I took my mama's worth, though somehow
I'm not the one holding it. I'm not sure
if I'll ever stop trying
to give it back.

But I

I was a sunny sprite, turning
rocks to jewels with my magic eyes.

I was Curious George, finding
every secret wonder.

I was Princess Ariel, singing
of perfect love from plastic pools.

I was pastel April, waiting
for a wonderful life to begin.

INTRUSIVE MEMORIES: SCENE 3 BLOOMINGTON, INDIANA, FRONT SEAT OF A GOLD '95 SATURN S1 - SPRING 1998 - AFTERNOON

She (7yo) sits in the passenger seat next to Mama (29yo). Mama wears a heavy expression. As they drive, the angled afternoon sun flashes through the passing trees like a strobe. Mama speaks with a hushed and low tone, attempting to sound casual. Yet, her voice shakes as it holds back waves of emotion at the end of each phrase.

MAMA:
How would you feel about going to live with your dad for a while?

HER:
Daddy? I miss him!

BACK TO:
Mama turns her face toward the driver's-side window to breathe through the lump in her throat as discreetly as possible. She doesn't know what she hoped for. Why she hopes at all. So she looks forward with resolve.

MAMA:
Okay, good. He can afford to give you more than I can.

CUT TO:
THE RADIO
Mama reaches for the knob on the radio. As her hand turns, the song's volume increases, as if this wall of sound could obscure her sorrow within the now too-small car, the now too-empty world.

Money

is all you need to buy a mother's arms. You don't need the whole mother—just the arms. You can strap them to her back. You can shackle the right arm to a minimum wage desk and watch the left arm reach for her baby. Money, it's a gas. Like steering a massive ship by its slender sail, you can seize the whole mother by just her hands. You can make her sit on them. Eventually her baby's cries will become the sound of her own helplessness. And just like that, for the price of a mother's arms, her dignity, like a coupon to entice future purchases, is tossed into the bag with the receipt. To maximize your investment, you should consider your other costless opportunities. For example, the baby. Without the mother's shielding forearms and clawed thrashes, the baby is practically free. Words are also free. Slip as many as you'd like into the baby's ear. The baby will repeat them to the hollow mother. The baby will love you for it.

How would you like
to relinquish your child?

a) explain they're a pawn in a larger game
b) admit you can't do anything to stop it
c) give them the ~~burden~~ illusion of choice

submit

How to survive a narcissist

As a child, I was sure quicksand
would be one of my biggest problems.
I saw all the illustrations,
the step-by-step escape plans:

Crawl on your belly.
Call for help.
Make no sudden movements.
The harder you kick,
the faster you'll sink.

Had I read these warnings
with the right title, maybe
I never would have slipped
chest-deep into the slurping
eager jaw of the world.

"smoke and mirrors" means "you and me," but at least I'm not on fire.

Maybe I was lovely,
but certainly
I was delicate
before you
shattered me.

If I was lovely
I forget
a little more each day

the shape I took
before I became
these pieces.

You could tell me
I was anything,
and I would need

oh

I would need

to believe you.

And you do,
and I did.

You say all kinds of things
about what I am
s u p p o s e d to be.
You'd have me think
at my best I am
a mirror.

As mirrors do, perhaps
I showed you something:

you would only ever
look at me
if it meant you could see

yourself.

Mother, men—

do they split us all
in two?
Do you feel
like separate pieces—
befores and afters,
too?

Embers & Words

You are a pretty girl
with a fat girl dying
to get out.

"Pretty" and "fat"
are meant to be
opposites, yet
I'm somehow both
and neither.

You should be more like the girl
who rides her bike everyday
in our neighborhood.
She is fit and tan, and you
would look like her if
you rode your bike more.

My appearance is my value.
I should be more like
anyone who does anything
differently than me.

From now on, when you think
you're hungry, ask me first
if *I'm* hungry. If I am,
that means you can eat.
If I'm not hungry,
you shouldn't be either.

My hunger is shameful.
My pangs are helpless.
Satiety is a forbidden thing.
My body is wrong
about her own needs.

You do not love me.
If you did you wouldn't hide
in your room so much.
And you'd do better
to do what I ask of you
so we wouldn't need
to keep having these
intense conversations.

People won't know
I love them
if I don't obey.
Love cannot exist
with boundaries, and
you hurt me
because I earn it.

If you cry like this
for your future husband
when he's trying to have
a serious conversation
he will want to hit you.
And, depending on who he is,
he might actually do it.

I'll never truly be safe
when I express my feelings.
The world is harsh, and
I am too soft for it.

All men are pigs,
and they will all
want to have sex with you.
When one someday
says he loves you
he won't truly mean it.

I cannot be
genuinely loved
because in this society
I'm just a woman,
and hungry men
are my only fate.

I always knew
you'd be a fox in bed
because of how much
you wanted to cuddle
when you were little.

Touch is only ever
a sexual invitation,
and I am only ever
a sexual animal.

I'll never tell you
how smart and awesome
I actually think you are
because I don't want you
to get a big head.

Confidence is the same
as arrogance, and both
are equally off-putting.
I won't be desired
until I stop finding myself
desirable.

My friends feel uncomfortable
and avoid eye contact with you
because of how beautiful
you're becoming.

I should hide
if I don't want people
to look at me like that.
My body makes
everyone uncomfortable—
but no one more so
than me.

You and your friends
laugh too much.
I don't like it when you
bring her over because
all you two do
is giggle.

My joy is obnoxious.
I should keep it
and the ones who amplify it
hidden.

You say "I love you"
too much, and it's starting
to mean less to me
each time.

Love and words
are currency.
Keep them scarce
to avoid inflation.

Lies & other lip syncs

When I listened closely
to Gordon Lightfoot, he
never said I was safe to lay
my head on anyone's
cold shoulders.

James Taylor says
they'll take your soul,
and Gordon says
they will grow old
          without ever being sorry.

James told me
I got a friend,
but my father was only
lip syncing.

In other words, be wary
of voiceless men who wrap
their lips around someone
else's truth.

INTRUSIVE MEMORIES: SCENE 4 INDIANAPOLIS, INDIANA, OPEN SUBURBAN GARAGE - SUMMER 2004 - LATE EVENING

They sit in the open garage of their home with the summer night sounds pouring in from the quiet suburban street. He (35yo) squats flat-footed, elbows resting on his knees, his arms hanging straight in front him, wrists slack, a Marlboro Light held loosely between his right thumb and forefinger. He takes a long and eager draw, his gray-blue eyes seeing past the world as he gathers his thoughts. She (14yo) sits on a cinderblock across from him—her usual spot for these familiar conversations. Waiting silently.

CUT TO:
HIM
When it comes to your mom, you're never going to come first in her life. Other men will always be her priority because she has no self-esteem, and they give her the validation she needs. You'll never be able to give that to her. And it's unfortunate, because she tends to date really shitty men: myself being the first of 'em. And I'll have to live with that for the rest of my life ... knowing that I knew her when she was at her best, and I ruined a good woman. Your relationship with her is completely upside-down because of it. She shouldn't be asking you for relationship advice or approval. And it might always be that way. And I know I'm partially to

blame for it. That's why I want to put everything I can into parenting you. Your mom is going to keep putting her broken feelings first, so I have to do the work of two parents.

Now I

am Amun-Ra, among
the old and forgotten gods.

I am Devil's Trumpet, rarely
blooming, hardly seen.

I am Eden's Eve, accepting
wrath so I can eat.

I am Castor and Pollux, a dual
spirit, split and burning.

I can still see you twirling my shoelaces.

One night in your garage
I told you I had prayed
to die. And you fell
to my feet, gagging between
your counter-prayers
as if your belief
in a god who would answer me
was stuck in your throat.

My shoelaces,
your beadless rosaries,
fell limp between
your Marlboro fingers.

I should go finish my homework.
        I would have said.

How could I have been your altar
of retching worship
and a child at the same time?
        I'd say now.

But instead, my neurons burned
two new beliefs, branded:
        I never want to see your remorse
        again, and god, apparently,
        doesn't take much convincing
        to kill.

Ashes, a la Carly Simon

Ashes, inherently
are a frail second life
of anything ruined
by fire. But

if ashes were convinced
they were born like this
they'd also think fire
was their god. And

I'm sure fire
would prefer it that way—
for ashes to never think
of themselves without also
worshiping the blaze
that ~~ruined~~ made them. But,

I remember being born—
the waning gibbous moon,
the blood of my mother,
the magic and bone,
the creation I was
before your flame ever scraped
my paper-pink skin.

I'm sure you think you made me,
as sure as I bet
you think this book
is about you,
don't you?

ASH, concluded

When we leave it to the fire
to say what we've become
the answer only benefits
its burning—
ashes—only ashes, it hisses
as its smoke obscures
our water from our sight.

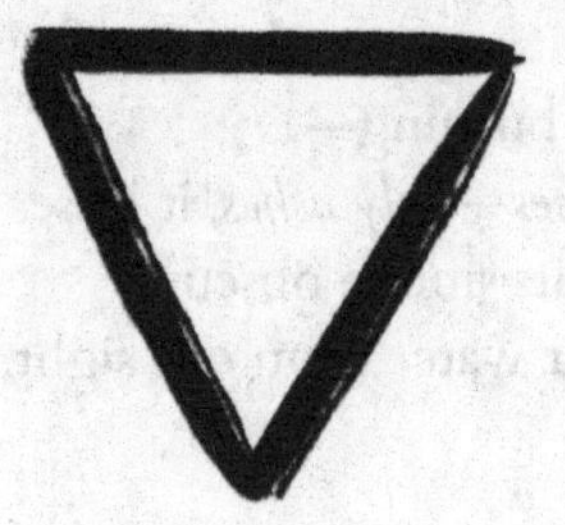

water

But we feel our water swell
undulating, inextinguishable
pain and healing both
cracking us open
like thunder
into an unsightly spill—
our own liquid iron
and salt.

INTRUSIVE MEMORIES: SCENE 5 SUBURBAN INDIANA, LIVING ROOM - 2000 - NIGHT

She (10yo) sits cross-legged on the floor by the couch, facing him where he (31yo) lays on his side, propped up on his right elbow. She laughs heartily at the joke he just made, head thrown back, hands pressed into her lap. She suddenly looks down to notice he is not laughing with her anymore.

CUT TO:
His eyes are fixed on her mouth. A joyful expression slowly drifts from his face, turning subtly into a look of concern and then disgust.

BACK TO:
She becomes curious and a bit worried. Her face fades quickly from a laugh to a smile, from a smile to something less.

HIM:
We've *got* to get your teeth fixed.

HER:
Oh … sorry.

CUT TO:
She quickly covers her mouth and averts her eyes from him. She learns that it's difficult for two people to smile wildly at the same time—that is, as long as she's one of those people.

My crooked necklace

I used to smile without thought,
and I wonder what it looked like. I bet
it was like a row of white opals
glistening behind the propped-up lid
of a treasure chest.

What if someone had given me
an opal necklace
for my tenth birthday
with a card that said *darling,*
I just love it when you laugh?

Patriarchy's Gamble

It turns out:
everything that yields
a submissive woman
can also create
a feminist.

Keep telling me to be quiet.

Then pull the lever and see
if you'll get cherries
or bombs.

Lightning

Mama, I figured it out.
We can go back in time
and put lightning in
your belly after all—
all I have to do
is become something
electric now.

INTRUSIVE MEMORIES: SCENE 6 SUBURBAN INDIANA, THE KITCHEN - 2006 - EVENING

She (16yo) is washing dishes in a sink full of soapy water. Her lips are pursed with visible but restrained fury. Her movements are steady and controlled. He (37yo) leans on the counter immediately to her left. His facial expression mirrors hers as he waits for her to give a response to the diatribe he just finished. But she says nothing.

HIM:
Do you know how much I want to hit you right now?

CUT TO:
She throws the plate into the sink, soapy water splashing onto them both and turns to face him. As if he just clipped the leash on her rage, she now wears an utterly abandoned stare.

HER:
Fucking do it then!

BACK TO:
His eyes sharpen. His lips tighten. He continues to stare at her. Through her.

CUT TO:
She waits as heavy seconds pass. When he does nothing, she turns to resume washing the dishes, faster now than before. Still, he looms. Until suddenly he walks away.

Idle hands, devil's tongue

I wish you would speak
with the back of your hand
or never at all.

But I'll bet my left cheek
you are the kind of coward who
only strikes in invisible ways.

While I long for sticks and stones,
you throw the sharper things—

words upon
words upon
words.

Embers & Words, Pt 2

You are a pretty girl
with a fat girl dying
to get out.

And you are an abuser
who believes he is kind
because he used the word
"pretty"
in a sentence.

You should be more like
the girl who rides her bike …

I am busy becoming
more like the person
in front of you.
And it isn't my fault
you haven't noticed.

You do not love me.
If you did, we wouldn't need
to have these conversations.

There are Olympic long jumpers
who don't travel as far
in a moment
as you did with your conclusion
that your berating me means
I'm the one who doesn't
love *you*.

If you cry like this
for your future husband,
he will want to hit you.

There is at least one person
whose thumb is the perfect shape
for my tears.
I'll introduce you someday,
but it shouldn't be a surprise
when their emotional intelligence
terrifies you, and you inevitably
just threaten to hit them.

All men are pigs.
When one someday says
he loves you,
he won't truly mean it.

The world of love is larger
than all men being like you
and all women only
wanting men.

I always knew you'd be
a fox in bed ...

You can't keep saying
you're nothing like
your incestuous father.

My friends feel uncomfortable
because of how beautiful
you are becoming.

I was born beautiful,
so nothing changed.
But now I understand
it isn't my beauty
your friends are
ashamed of.

You say "I love you"
too much.

You're right.
You don't deserve it.

Diagnostic and Statistical Manual of Mental Disorders, fifth edition

I left your childhood vinyls
in a thrift store bin
for someone else to sort through
much like how you left
the breadcrumbs of my childhood
scattered within
the DSM-5.

My abuser

Took me to 45 of the 50 states before I was 18
(performed parenthood)

Learned I was good company
(was surprised I had a personality)

Taught me how to swim
(threw me in the opaque lake and waited)

Told me I was beautiful
(like stacking blocks before wrecking them)

Paid for a third of my undergrad
(then leveraged it for my compliance)

Paid for a lot of things, actually
(tightening my leash to his post)

Thought I was a magic well
(and I don't disagree)

Showed me off to others
(as you would a trophy)

Gave me my own computer
(and spied on it)

Let me decorate my bedroom
(but forbade it as my sanctuary)

Let me keep the cat
(then killed her when I wouldn't come home)

Taught me to never quit
(against his own benefit)

Made me laugh a million times
(charisma, like a fishing reel)

Laughed at my jokes, too
(I come by it honestly)

Danced in the living room
(he was a vivacious creature)

Is a human being
(with a father worse than mine)

In other words, it's rarely obvious.

A trauma bond
is like an asteroid
which becomes a meteor
which becomes a crater
which becomes a void
which fills up with water
and becomes a lake
so you can't call it a void
anymore.

INTRUSIVE MEMORIES: SCENE 7
SUBURBAN INDIANAPOLIS
SUMMER 2011 - DUSK

They sit in the backyard of their home on sun-bleached patio furniture. The kitchen begins to light the concrete patio through the sliding doors as dusk falls. She (21yo) has her back to the house, facing him (42yo). The trees slowly become silhouettes behind him as dusk falls. The air is the kind of temperature you almost can't feel.

HIM:
My leadership comes with privileges but also responsibility. You can't in good faith tell me that you want a father in your life and then not accept my leadership when I offer it to you. That boy did not go through the appropriate channels to get proper access to you. He can't possibly be "the one" if he doesn't have the wisdom and honorable principles to come to me first. You're worth more than that. There's nothing he can do to make me respect him after he missed the opportunity to be upfront and ask me for my blessing to court you. You can't call me your father and then not follow me. If you want a father who takes care of you, leads you, helps you pay for school, and is there for you, you can have it. But you can't have all those things and then disobey me by continuing to see him.

CUT TO:
HER
She already left her body. She sits expressionless, dreading the moment he'll inevitably expect her to speak. As silence builds, pressure mounts in her chest. The more it rises, the more asleep she feels inside. But she reaches inward. Finds words inside of her like a stray thread and pulls it upward. Finally her words slip quietly from her soulless husk of a body.

HER:
It sounds like, no matter what I do, I won't have the kind of father I need.

CUT TO:
HIM
Like lightning whipping the earth, his composure cracks. He raises up and thrusts his chair far behind him in one startling and swift motion. The pale cushion tumbles out as the chair falls on its side. His face is red and contorted with an instant display of rage. He begins to pace.

CUT TO:
HER HANDS
She's cold yet sweaty as she winces and grips the chair beneath her body, waiting for whatever word or object might be thrown next.

The manners of wanting

Artistry:
1. cherish beauty
2. create new beauty in its likeness
3. leave the muse as you found her
4. this is your worship
5. the alchemy of your gratitude

Thievery:
1. cherish beauty
2. pluck it from its place
3. remember a stolen thing can always be stolen again
4. this is your undoing
5. why loveliness wilts in your hand

INTRUSIVE MEMORIES: SCENE 8a SUBURBAN INDIANAPOLIS SUMMER 2011 - NIGHT

He (42yo) sits at her computer desk in her bedroom. He scrolls through her private messages while his new wife (38yo) stands faithfully behind him, her small, manicured hands delicately rested on top of the desk chair by his shoulders.

She (21yo) stands barefoot in the doorway. She's wearing her pajamas - a black tank top and bright yellow boxers with a vibrant ladybug print. She clutches her phone against her stomach, her posture clenched and still. It feels like forever until his words, clipped and few, surgically slice the silence open like a scalpel.

HIM:
How long has this been going on? I told you to drop him.

CUT TO:
HER
She becomes pale and light-headed. She opens her mouth to speak, but - she's going to throw up. She darts into the bathroom across the hall, slams her palm onto the light switch, then heaves into the toilet. Hot bile - she forgot she hadn't eaten.

CUT TO:
THE MIRROR
She stands to turn on the faucet, then makes eye contact with herself in the mirror - a pale and terrified stranger. Where does her blood go when it leaves her face like this? Adrenaline throbs in her ears against the loud hum-rush of the overhead fan and running faucet. The sounds become the new walls and ceiling of a suddenly too-tight room. Is her phone charged?

CUT TO:
THE PHONE
23%
No Messages

CUT TO:
THE MIRROR
She looks again at the mirrored stranger and disowns the reflection. She can't be this person. She looks at the toilet. If she flushes it, he will hear it. And then he'll expect to see her return shortly after. But now he's had time to think and prepare his arguments. No. She absolutely can't go back. Not when her thoughts are still too shallow and buzzing.

CUT TO:
THE BATHROOM DOOR
She slowly slips through the gently cracked door—the fan and faucet still running behind her, her stomach still in the toilet, and her fear, as if a spell was cast, left entirely with the stranger in the mirror.

He taught me to abandon myself.

I cast the traits of my father into what will be
a former version of me, once I burn her like

an effigy. How many times have I died, exactly
like this, at my own hands, without burial or fond

eulogy? Instead, I turn my shoulder away from
each of my past selves. And this manner, this manner

of disowning, is one I first learned from him. Yet,
I tell myself I'm nothing like him, as if

it isn't exactly this slaughter and shoulder
that makes me my father's daughter.

INTRUSIVE MEMORIES: SCENE 8b
SUBURBAN INDIANAPOLIS
SUMMER 2011 - NIGHT

CUT TO:
THE FRONT DOOR
She turns the knob so slowly, then stealthily slides through the second and final cracked door of her abandoned home. She gingerly closes it behind her. When she hears the quiet and confirming click of the latch, she turns and launches into a sprint.

CUT TO:
HER FEET
She takes unpredictable turns, tearing through various backyards to reach adjacent neighborhoods. Her bare feet smack pavement, then grass, then mud or maybe dogshit as she races through another stranger's yard. Her shins collect dewy cutlets of grass as she races. If she doesn't know where she is, he won't either.

CUT TO:
HER
She finds a dark cul-de-sac, picks a house on the right, and stealthily darts into its side yard. The yard slopes down into a steep hill. She swiftly throws herself prone on the slope - she can't be seen from the road here. Her heart pounds against the damp earth.

CUT TO:
TEXT MESSAGE:
"Malia, are you free? I need someone to pick me up, it's urgent. I can't go home tonight."
"Are you okay???"
"I'm safe. Can you come? I'm so sorry."
"I'm coming! Tell me where to find you in 30 minutes."

(12 Missed Calls: Dad)
(Incoming Call: Dad)
(17%)

CUT TO:
THE ROAD
She hears the crackling of slow tires on pavement. The light from a pair of approaching headlights raises shadows of trees and mailboxes upon the neighboring houses.

CUT TO:
HER
Her heart pounds in her ears. She closes her mouth to suppress her loud and labored breathing. She closes her eyes tightly and presses her right cheek to the grass.

CUT TO:
THE SOUNDS
No car doors. No voices. No footsteps. Just a mediocre rumble and rev from the road, progressively fading into a familiar night silence.

A lazy breeze whispering to the leaves.
Crickets calling and responding in rhythmic chats.
A dying streetlamp buzzing its final words.

CUT TO:
HER
She expels a long breath and slowly opens her eyes. But she's met with a vision that shocks every muscle and breath into another frozen stillness.

CUT TO:
THE HOME
The spot she'd chosen is only four feet away from a low window, allowing a shockingly clear and voyeuristic view into the home next to her.

She sees a dark and unoccupied living room, spacious and well-decorated. Only the flickering blue light from the forgotten television illuminates the tossed blankets and pillows on the couch, the empty glasses and open books on the table. Signs of comfort. Signs of safety. Further inside, only one room is lit and occupied - the dining room. A happy family eats a late dessert together at the table.

She weeps.

Mothers

One chain runs the line
of my mothers,
ankle to ankle, generations
shuffling, believing
every word their fathers said.

Mother,
in 1990 I twisted
in your stomach.
I pressed against
the walls and cried *surely*
the key to your shackles
is hidden in
your mouth?

Mother,
I have a father too.
His words clipped my tongue,
and as my belly filled with blood, I ran
away from him,
away from our line
of mothers
who believed every word
their fathers said.

Generations

Waves lick the debris
along the coastline
pulling wreckage back,
rolling it forward again.
And this is how it happens—
how eternal effort covers
no distance. Hurt daughters become
hurt mothers, can only see themselves in
hurting men, so they breed perfectly hurting daughters,
and god, does it feel as rough as dying,
to be anything other than *hurt*
in this corrosive tide? So
we lather with lye,
burn, rinse,
repeat.

Heartbreak has many sounds

and I thought I'd heard them all:
the clang and clamor
of cacophonous griefs,
the crunch of a fragile thing
under a settled weight,
the silence that haunts, replaces,
the marrow of my ribs.

But my mother-wound ripped quietly
like wet paper in my chest
slow and soft and tender,
an already saturated thing: my hope
torn silently as a breath.

This is the truth
every daughter must swallow:
only we can save ourselves.

But my next realization hangs
too dry in my throat:
my mother is a daughter too.

Parentification

My kids would do better than me, I'm sure. Maybe
they'd have less debt or less time
between when they're born and when they're alive.
But as I wait for my own mama
to heal, I'd surely
pass my bitter tea, and burn
the hands of my baby. Someday, I'd open
my mouth, and salt would fall out
instead of sugar. Because that's what happens
when people become parents,
when they were never first a child.

Capital J

I am afraid
of my laugh lines,
the shape of my mouth,
and the way I write
my capital Js.

I thought about how doggedly
I try to believe
I am good—
        something else my father
        and I have in common.

Am I a narcissist?
I asked my therapist.

This time she
didn't answer my question
with another question.

But a narcissist might be good
at convincing their therapist
they aren't a narcissist, so
I still couldn't find sleep.

Months later my cat
became sick. I held his
begging body. I rocked,
and I realized my need
to believe in my goodness
is Justified.

Because he looked at me like a god
and cried to me like a god,
and I realized what I'd do
if I were a god—
and for the first time I was desperate
to become one.

A non-comprehensive list of my 2020 Google searches

How to tell if your father was a sociopath
Can sociopaths feel love
Is sociopathy genetic
Indianapolis obituaries
How to know if your parent is still alive when you're estranged
Difference between a sociopath and narcissist
Can cats catch COVID
Would I have to quarantine from my cats if I got COVID
What is a narcopath
Signs of narcissistic abuse
What is the mother wound
Enmeshment in mother relationships
Twitch reset password link
Louisville COVID deaths today
Am I a narcissist
Free therapists in Louisville
Cheap therapists in Louisville
Therapists in Louisville
Therapists
How to do moss stitch, easy crochet video
Gov Beshear COVID talk today
Who is Gov Beshear's ASL interpreter
Virginia Moore bio
Signs of PTSD
What is C-PTSD
Can you have PTSD if you don't have visual flashbacks
What are emotional flashbacks
How to write an obituary
N95 masks Amazon
Body Keeps the Score book reviews

Therapists in Louisville
What is EMDR
Does EMDR work
What is financial abuse
Signs of spiritual abuse
What is emotional incest
Can you be suicidal even if you're afraid of killing yourself
Theater showtimes tomorrow

Women and Witches

Before my mother's mother
was a mother
or a wife or
a fiancée or girlfriend
she was her own girl:
a girl in the summer who
once wore shorts too short, so,
her mother
washed her legs with lye.
Petite pillars of autonomy became
sheared of hair, and will,
and so she learned her lesson—
the lesson of women and witches
taught forever
before my mother's mother
was an embryo or a shadow
of a thought in her father:

to be seen
is to burn.

Water, Concluded

Flames finally
sizzle under our storm, and
we'd almost believe
we are safe from the fire
of our past. But the floods
and tempests in our chests
are a suffering of their own,
our ashes and water swirling
into LYE.

The fire may be gone, but
we still burn.
Stripped
but not yet
clean.

oil

Surely
we pressed enough
sacred oil,
softness, from
these hard moments?
So let's caress it deeply
into our unloved parts—
the cleansing and cooling
relief of not just recovery
but healing.

How would you like to burn?

a) As a condemned woman, strapped to a post, stoked and prodded by fearful men
b) As a weakened structure, folding to ember, kissing its knees in death
c) As lye, the toxic chemical strip, a compounding heat, one ingredient short of relief
d) As the sun, a veritable thing, in merciless wielding, a dangerous but necessary light

submit

Eye Movement Desensitization and Reprocessing

I wiggle my thumb, deepening
        my grip
                until I reach the soil, then

further
        until I touch the roots,
                like neurons, transmitting

beliefs that no longer
        serve me.
                I pull

from the amygdala,
        hippocampus,
                fear and memory.

I break
        the electricity of it.
                And once I do

I realize I can plant
        any new seeds
                I want.

Hope

What grows
in the garden
at the end of the world?

Do you think it is anything
we haven't already seen?

May I be both death and doula

of all that passes through me?
May I tenderly coax out
the stillborn griefs
my lifeless beliefs
while blessing them with quiet
honor?
May I swipe shut the eyelids
of the aches I have mothered
the losses I was never to keep?

I Am: Redux

I am the sunny sprite, changing
rocks to jewels
with my glittery perspective.

I am Curious George, finding
peace in unanswerable
questions.

I am Princess Ariel, after
recovering my voice and leaving
the weight of water behind.

I am pastel April, knowing
every death is its own
beginning.

I am Amun-Ra, creator
of my own bright and
terrifying world.

I am Devil's Trumpet, only
blossoming when my needs
are met.

I am Eden's Eve, free
from ignorant fruit and man's
abandonment.

I am Castor and Pollux, both
celestial
and never alone.

I, (your name here),

hereby remit my believed ability to control how I am perceived or treated by others.

I understand that my value is an inherent and immovable thing: incapable of increasing or decreasing in response to the way others feel about me or how I feel about myself.

I understand that my emotions are meant to alert me to my own inner workings. While my feelings are true, they are not harbingers of Truth itself. I swear not to ignore my feelings nor to abandon my responsibility as their tender and capable caretaker. I accept this responsibility proudly, and I shall never forfeit it to another.

Similarly, I absolve myself of all responsibility for the feelings, decisions, and fate of others. I understand that the ones I love must save themselves, just as my saving is by my own hand.

I understand that I have the power to set an example but not to change minds. I swear never to waste effort on convincing someone to love me, begging someone to see me, or performing for expectations that don't align with my own.

I choose the healing salve of softness over the fierce cauterization of rage. I choose the strength of vulnerability over the false fortress of resentment. I choose the bravery of self-acceptance over the fragility of self-defense. I choose new difficulties over the patterned pain of my ancestors.

I choose my agency over victimhood.

THE MAGICAL WELL was 30 years old when it was found dead on the afternoon of June 16, 2020. The well is survived by Narcissus, who grieves its waters and the shimmering reflection it provided, the Thirsty, who mourn its whetting relief, and the Wounded, who can no longer soak in its healing properties. The well lies buried under a grave marked by a single gray rock. Some speculate the well never died but that it can only be found by those who wish to replenish its magic. According to this folklore, those who desire only to consume from the well will be dismayed to find only a gray rock in its place. In fact, most do not find the rock at all due to its incredibly unremarkable features. While the well was fabled to slip siren songs into the ears and hearts of the lonely, the gray rock is ever, unnervingly, unresponsive. Never has an item been known to die so selectively. In kind, the well is grieved only by those who once benefited from its guardless giving.

Detachment

de·tach·ment
/də'taCHm(ə)nt/

noun

1. [a]the difference between an anchor and a hot air balloon, [b]the snapping line between one's history and one's definition, [c]the decision to act instead of react, [d]the *letting go* which precedes the *rising above*, [e]the moment one's decisions are made for the future instead of the past

ex: "She was surprised to discover it: detachment sounds nothing like the wet rip of heartbreak."

Freedom has many sounds

And I want to hear them all.
The whisper of a loving index
finger on my skin, the opening
of myself, like any oiled hinge,
the groaning
of a heavy door-turned-portal,
the wild breath
of my night garden, the clink
and shattering
of discarded locking keys
and with them, everything
that no longer turns
in me.

Craftsman

I am not a broken thing.
But gentle love
is as divine a truth
as the hell I've been to,
and careful hands
could teach me how
I might make myself
complete.

Scarcity

Sometimes I can feel
that cold home as if
I'm in it. The naked
walls and sun-bleached couch
yearning
for art and cotton drapes,
beauty and soft cover, the way
I yearned.

From my bedroom,
my chest and stomach
searched for anything
but each other to erode.

But now my lover's hand
finds my knee.
Their lips, my neck.
And in my ear, whispers
of love and other horrors,
describing every detail
of the magic that holds
my skin and the Milky Way
together.

Nostalgia is a grief

for the few things that were
perfect. I couldn't love
this fully if I'd never been emptied
before. Warriors forget
the reasons behind each scar but fall
asleep to memories of every
tender moment—and that's
what I mean
when I say you are welcome
to hurt me if you want to.

The only reality I know

is my own. Which means
you might have done your best,
and you might well be hurting, even after hurting
me. Maybe to you, I am the bloody-jowled hound
still holding what you need. But your reality
is yours to eat. It's never been a portion
slapped onto my plate nor a dripping kill
withheld between my teeth.

The Last Word

If my poetry were a virus
or supplication, this
is the moment I stop praying
over porcelain, when my back lifts
from the arc of its heaving reverence,
when I wipe the sweat of waiting
from my temple, and I exit,
finally godless, indifferent
to the confessions and tithes left
in the bowl.

If my torture ends,
if a tree falls in the forest,
am I still a poet?
Or is this foreign freedom
my next romanticized burden
a right hand suddenly freed,
ready to catch the sunshine?

Rust,

I run my fingers
across its roughness
and I remember
the grit of long
survival—the brittle fate
of all hardened things.

May I be the oil,
I say.

And with this spell,
my softness becomes
my safety.

Saponification, an epilogue

Only now can we wash
ourselves of the soot
that marked us
by combining
ashes, our grief,
with water, our reactions,
and finally with oil,
the levity of our real joy.

Notes

Sodium hydroxide is the chemical name for lye, an inorganic and caustic compound. In soapmaking, lye is formed by boiling ashes in water.

"Lies and other lip syncs" refers to lyrics contained in the songs, "You've Got a Friend," by James Taylor and, "Cold on the Shoulder," by Gordon Lightfoot.

"Ashes, a la Carly Simon" refers to the chorus of "You're So Vain" by Carly Simon.

Amun-Ra was Supreme of the Egyptian gods—a fusion between Amun, creator of the world, and Ra, god of the sun. Amun-Ra is written to have created both himself and the universe around him. He was often symbolized as a ram, representing both fertility and war—the power to create and also destroy life.

Devil's Trumpet is one of the many common names for Datura inoxia—also commonly referred to as moonflower, jimsonweed, or thorn-apple. It is widely known for its brief and temperamental blooms, which only occur during the night. Notably, all parts of Devil's Trumpet are poisonous. Despite this, it was brewed as a hallucinogenic tea within some Indigenous cultures to be used as a spiritual rite of passage.

Castor and Pollux were twin brothers in Greek mythology. Both sons of Leda, Castor was the mortal son of father Tynadareus, while Pollux was an immortal son of Zeus. The myth tells of Pollux requesting Zeus for the ability to share his immortality with his beloved brother, Castor. When this was granted, both twins were cast to the skies, becoming the two defining stars within the Gemini constellation.

"Alpha" and "Omega" refer to biblical verses such as Revelation 1:8 and Revelation 21:6, wherein Jesus calls himself "the Alpha and the Omega, the beginning and the end." Alpha and Omega are the first and last letters of the Greek alphabet. These terms are often used within Christianity to represent the dual and all-encompassing attributes of God—"first and last," "greatest and least."

EMDR stands for Eye Movement Desensitization and Reprocessing. This is a therapeutic practice similar to exposure therapy, which combines focus on traumatic memories with bilateral stimulation (such as eye movement or hand tapping) to trigger traumatic responses and reprocess them with more adaptive beliefs. Though debated, this is a common and research-based treatment for PTSD and other similar psychological conditions.

C-PTSD stands for Complex Post-Traumatic Stress Disorder. This diagnosis is not yet contained within the DSM-5 (Diagnostic and Statistical Manual of Mental Disorders, fifth edition) and is therefore debated as a legitimate diagnosis within psychotherapy. C-PTSD is believed to be caused by complex traumas (repeated and/or prolonged with little to no chance for escape) and shares many signs/symptoms (though not all) with PTSD. C-PTSD is thought to be marked by feelings of worthlessness, loss of identity, difficulty managing emotions, hypervigilance, and prolonged feelings of terror. If you relate to these experiences, please seek professional counseling and care: healing is real and available to you.

"The Magical Well" is inspired by Victoria Chang's "Obit."

Saponification is the process of making soap, wherein caustic lye is joined with softening agents, such as soluble fats or oil. May you enjoy the soft and lovely things of this world, accept them as your own, that your own cleansing from ash and lye may be complete.

Thank You

To Buv:

Once, it was easy
to know what to say. Good thing
love rests well in peace.

To Mama:

To meet your softness
is to learn there's more to strength
than ferocity.

To Justine:

You: a sturdy root
Our friendship: perennial
And I: stay grateful.

To my chosen family:

A bond formed without
your blood and obligation
is freer than pact.

To those I've lost:

Not to point fingers,
but your leaving softened me
more than staying could.

Acknowledgments

To Sarabande Books and Joy Priest for lending your mics and pages to the ready poets of Louisville and for granting my poem, "Frail," a home on page 115 of *Once A City Said—a Louisville Poets Anthology.*

To *Fatal Flaw Magazine* for including "When I say God is a woman, I mean" in its tenth issue: *WITNESS.*

To *Rogue Agent* for featuring "When did they stop asking about you Mama" in its 109th issue.

About the Author

Sunshine "Sunny" Lately (she/they) is a queer Kentuckiana poet who enjoyed a career as a speech-language pathologist before pursuing poetry. Whether as a poet or clinician, Sunshine believes in the restorative and contagious powers of self-expression. They are dedicated to sharing that power with others through their writing, community involvement, and writing workshop, Golden Hours.

Title Index

E

F

G

H

I

T

W

First Line Index

E

F

G

H

I

Y

www.ingramcontent.com/pod-product-compliance
Lightning Source LLC
LaVergne TN
LVHW030922080826
845145LV00013B/3014

* 9 7 8 1 5 9 4 9 8 2 1 9 4 *